CREATE A WINNING BUSINESS STRATEGY

Learn to create Successful Business Strategies to boost Growth

BERT LANGA

Copyright © 2018 Bert Langa

All rights reserved.

ISBN: 9781983098505

DEDICATION

To my family.

CONTENTS

Want a Successful Business? Build a Winning Business Strategy	3
Business Strategy Blueprint	7
Business Plan vs Business Strategy	12
Key Business Objectives	17
Market Data Analysis	21
Organic Growth Drivers	25
Market Penetration	28
Market Development	31
Solution Development	34
Diversification	36
How to document Organic Growth Drivers	37
Organic Growth Drivers: HealthApp example	40
Inorganic Growth Drivers	47
Enablers	50
The One Page Business Strategy	52
Business Strategy in the Real World	54
Financial Model	59
Global Action Plan	62
The answer to the Kodak problem	65
Conclusion	67
About the Author	68

ACKNOWLEDGMENTS

To my family

WANT A SUCCESSFUL BUSINESS? BUILD A WINNING BUSINESS STRATEGY

Hello, how are you? First, I would like to thank you for buying *"Business Strategy Formulation: Become a Strategy Consultant."* My name is Bert and for more than 20 years I worked as a consultant for one of the largest global consulting firms. Now I am a private investor and founder of different technology startups. Both experiences allow me to successfully find solutions to business problems for companies of any size, from startups to listed companies.

Throughout this book, we are going to discuss Business Strategies. To do this, we will start by defining the meaning of the work Strategy in a business context.

There are numerous books on the subject, although one of the most important definitions was created by Porter in 1996 (one of the most well-known strategists in the world), in a publication in the Harvard Business Review (*What Is Strategy?, Michael E. Porter, FROM THE NOVEMBER-DECEMBER 1996 ISSUE*). In it, Porter talks to us about Strategy as "a combination of objectives that the company focuses its efforts on, and the methods that used to reach said objectives".

However, in a subsequent article, Forbes magazine offers us a very practical and interesting definition that combines both words, Strategy and Business. It goes: "A strategy is a framework for making decisions about how you will play the game of business" (*What The Heck Is A Strategy Anyway?, Ann Latham, Oct 29, 2017*).

This simple definition brings up a question: have you ever wondered why certain businesses are more successful and have substantially better returns than average? In general terms, I can assure you that this success is due to having a Business Strategy that is well-defined and even better executed. In other words, these companies clearly define a framework that allows them to make decisions about the future state they want to reach and are beautifully executing their action plan to reach it.

During the process of defining this future state, the company designs the products and services they want to sell (both current and new), the clients and markets where they want to sell them (both current and new), they identify possible companies with which they want to establish relationships (or even buy), and, finally, they develop the components of the business that will be necessary for supporting the company's operations (called "enablers").

Below we will see different examples of leading companies that are disciplined in executing their business strategies in order to continue creating value and earning competitive advantages.

First, let's think about the process of Apple expanding to China several years ago. The company invested more than a billion dollars in this process. In other words, as part of their Business Strategy, Apple decided to improve the sale of their products and services in a new geographic market: China. And, to do this, they invested quite a fortune that has led to this region becoming one of the three best markets in terms of sales (according to Apple's data).

Now let's discuss Google's transformation into Alphabet. Logically, this chance was defined as part of their Business Strategy. What did they want to achieve with this? In the words of the company's leadership, it was intended to maintain the corporate and global management of the business while allowing for different business units with teams not working in areas exclusively related to IT to have greater flexibility (i.e. Healthcare). That is, they wanted their management to become more efficient and agile, since

Google's size was beginning to make continued innovation much more complicated.

Finally, let's talk about General Electric, which, as part of its Business Strategy, decided several years ago to enter the 3D printing business. To do this, it invested $1.4 billion into buying various companies that were leaders in this technology. This type of purchasing is called inorganic growth (as opposed to organic growth through the company's products and services). I'll discuss this later in more detail.

In other words, Business Strategy is a framework that allows us to make decisions regarding how to manage the business in order to continue bringing value to our clients. In the case of Apple, the target entailed expanding to China; at Google, the segmentation of the company's operations; and for GE, it was necessary to enter into the 3D printing market.

In any of the previous examples, the executives responsible for developing the Business Strategy used a specific process. In this book, I will explain this method, a series of actions that will allow you to reach the desired growth rates faster than your competitors.

In order to do this, in the first part of the book, we will discuss the importance of correctly defining business objectives.

Later on, I will explain in detail how to develop a Market Analysis.

Once we know our objectives and market potential, we will focus on defining the key components of the Business Strategy: organic and inorganic growth drivers, and the enablers.

To put into practice everything we have learned, we will review the business strategies of several listed companies. We will also develop a complete case study for a technology startup that sells mobile applications in healthcare.

Finally, you will learn how to develop a Financial Model (where the expected investments and benefits are defined) and the Action Plan in order to implement the Business Strategy.

This process for developing business strategies is based on my experience developing management projects for the most widely-known listed companies (although the method that I will explain can be used for smaller companies and even startups –in fact, the main case study is for a startup called HealthApp.

Knowing this method will allow you to become a market leader capable of:

—Understanding the current position of your company and defining where you want to go.

—Identifying the key steps needed for carrying out the defined strategy.

—Encouraging discussion and internal debate in your work teams.

—Properly structuring complex problems and being able to solve them.

—Organizing information from multiple sources in order to obtain relevant data.

—And, ultimately, delivering better results.

Finally, before moving on to the next chapter, I wanted to ask you to solve a puzzle. Do you remember the multinational company Kodak? In 2001, 3.12 billion rolls of photo film were sold worldwide. At that time, Kodak had a 40% market share, Fuji had 26% and Agfa had 13%; however, in 2012, only 11 years later, Kodak filed for bankruptcy. Can you tell me why? At the end, I will give you the answer to this question.

BUSINESS STRATEGY BLUEPRINT

The process for developing a Business Strategy (Business Strategy Blueprint or BSB) is a holistic method based on the knowledge I have acquired as management consultant. The following graph represents the activities this entails:

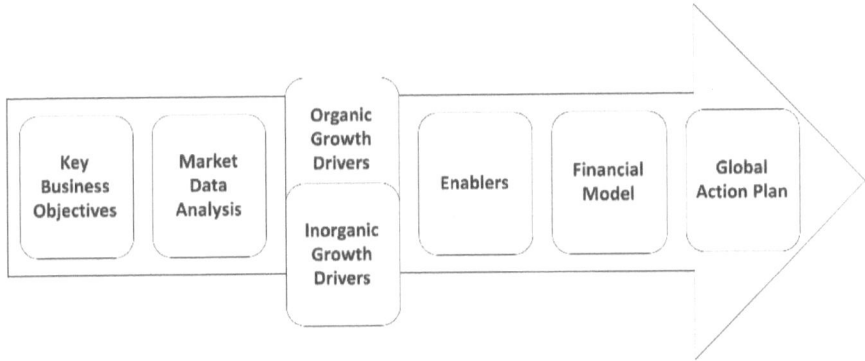

First, The Key Business Objectives must be identified, which can fall under different perspectives:

—Financial: growth objectives (e.g. sales, revenue, or profitability).

—Client: level of impact and relevance for the end customers (e.g. market positioning, market share).

—Internal: efficiency and effectiveness in the internal operations of the business (e.g. cost optimization, process flexibility, automation level, etc.).

—Talent: level of success in the managing and motivating work teams (e.g. level of employee satisfaction with the company).

Next, a Market Analysis is created for where the company operates and its positioning in said market. This means knowing where we are starting and, more importantly, the challenges our clients face that will guide the Business Strategy.

Then, the organic and inorganic growth drivers that will allow you to reach objective global growth.

When defining the growth strategies that will be part of the business strategy, we can opt for these two possibilities: organic or inorganic growth. Defining how we want to grow is one of the main responsibilities of a good strategist, given that the decisions we make will have a direct influence on the results of the company and its employees.

Organic growth means pursuing growth based on the company's current assets and/or the creation of new ones (although always taking advantage of internal capabilities). This is the usual way to grow SMEs or SMBs. For example, the development of new products/services or geographical expansion.

Inorganic growth is based on mergers, acquisitions or strategic alliances with third parties (later on I will go into these concepts in detail). That is, it relies on the involvement of other companies.

In addition to these growth drivers, the Enablers must be defined. These are actions that affect the entire company and favor the achievement of non-financial business objectives. They are called Enablers because, together with the Growth Drivers, they make the Business Strategy a reality.

The next step is to define the Financial Model that will support the achievement of the financial objectives (sales/revenue/profitability). The aim is to answer the following questions: what investments are necessary to make the Business Strategy a reality? What return will be gained in terms of increased sales, revenue and profitability?

Finally, the Global Action Plan is defined, including all the steps needed for implementing the Business Strategy and achieving the set objectives. The steps may affect different areas—for example, employees, revenue, or marketing.

It seems difficult, but it is not. Although in coming sections we will take a detailed look at specific case studies, below we will apply the BSB to develop the business strategy for a company that works to implement cybersecurity solutions.

Imagine an American company—we'll call it CyberLog—which has been selling customized Cybersecurity solutions to the needs of SMBs since 2008. For several years, the company has seen growth stagnate and is now starting to see losses. Customers mostly complain about a low quality after-sales service and low level of specialization.

For this reason, the members of the Board have decided to develop a new strategy that will allow them to grow again. Can you tell me which business objective perspective should guide the new Strategy? It's clearly from a financial perspective. The main objective is "to grow."

As in all of our books, this case study is based on a real project and company. As such, the team that developed the Business Strategy defined different key business objectives in terms of growth (financial perspective).

First, they wanted to increase the volume of revenue per customer from $25,000 to $40,000. They also wanted to increase profitability of sales up to an EBITDA (gross operating profit calculated before deducting financial expenses) of 16%.

Finally, the Board also determined specific objectives that fell under the Client perspective. Specifically, they wanted to increase the client portfolio from 2,460 to 3,500 customers.

Once the business objectives were defined, they determined the organic and inorganic growth drivers and the Enablers. Although I will explain the method for doing this the correct way later on (for example, using the Ansoff matrix), here is a sample of the resulting strategy for this area.

At the level of organic growth drivers, it was determined that a specific Cybersecurity solution for SAP ERP environments would be created and sold. Companies that use SAP need this software to be completely secure in terms of availability, authenticity, confidentiality, and integrity. Creating a specific solution for this would allow them to expand the customer base, profitability, and average revenue (the key objectives of their strategy).

At the level of inorganic growth drivers, they decided to lock down a strong alliance with a leading SAP distributor and installer in the American SMB market. Can you imagine why? Obviously, the idea was to sell the new cybersecurity product to all that company's customers under a revenue sharing agreement.

Let's now move on to the Enablers; for example, the implementation of a corporate CRM solution that would allow a more efficient management of the clients and, more importantly, of the after-sales services.

The next two sections of the Business Strategy require a rigorous and extensive amount of work in order to define the Financial Model and the Action Plan.

At the financial level, the team obtained a model that determined the need for a $5 million investment with an expected return on investment (ROI) of thirty-two months.

On the other hand, the Global Action Plan included the tasks from the Growth Drivers and the Enablers; for example, the creation of a new business unit with specific responsibilities for selling the new SAP product, the execution of a specific marketing campaign gain recognition in that market segment, and the implementation of the new CRM corporate solution.

As you have seen in this case study, the BSB application is not complex. It is a structured and simple way to understand the *Why* (the key business objectives and market positioning), the *How* (the growth drivers, enablers, and financial model), and the *What* (the action plan) of a business strategy.

Next, we will review each of the components of the BSB in detail. However, first I will explain the main differences between two strategic planning exercises that are often confused: the Business Strategy and the Business Plan.

BUSINESS PLAN VS BUSINESS STRATEGY

As I explained before, the Strategy is a framework for making decisions about how you will manage your business. In short, the Business Strategy tries to answer different questions.

First, there are those related to the Why:

—What are my business objectives and indicators for measuring compliance?

—What is my current market positioning?

—What is my starting point to achieve these goals?

Then, there are those related to the How:

—What current solutions (mix of products and services) should I boost in order to achieve the desired growth rates?

—What new solutions should I create to achieve the desired growth rates?

—Should I expand geographically? In which countries/continents/markets? Is it an option to expand to emerging markets?

—What are the enablers that will help the Business Strategy to be executed successfully?

—What financial planning is needed to achieve the objectives (sales and investments)?

And, finally, those related to the What:

—What action plan should I execute?

As you can see, the Business Strategy is a structured method that allows you to define a specific action plan to achieve the defined objectives.

However, it is an exercise in strategic planning that is different from developing of the Business Plan. In this section, we will analyze the differences between the Business Plan and the Business Strategy. In principle, it might seem like they are both the same since both are meant for business development and growth. Actually, the Business Strategy is often confused with the Business Plan. This occurs mainly in startups, where the need to develop a business plan for convincing investors is confused with the need to develop a business strategy for growing an existing business.

In this sense, there is a key word that differentiates the Business Strategy from the Business Plan. That word is "create"—whether a company is created or not. In other words, beyond academic definitions, Strategy is used to develop existing businesses and the Plan is used to create them.

In addition, the key issues to be analyzed in both planning exercises are different (although part of the analysis carried out in the Plan can be reused for the Strategy). Below we will describe the different components of the Business Plan and its ability to influence or be reused when creating the Business Strategy.

Let's start with the Mission: the definition of the company's reason for being (which refers to the present). This definition is a key piece of information that should be reviewed when defining the Business Strategy.

Next is the Vision: the aspirations for the company's future (which refers to the medium-long term). This definition is also a key piece of information that should be reviewed when defining the Business Strategy.

Let's now turn to the Strategic Objectives of the Business Plan (in terms of growth, positioning, etc.). The Business Strategy must be governed by these objectives and they should be updated, if applicable.

Next, the Business Plan includes an analysis of the environment made up of the PEST Factor Analysis (Political, Technological, Social and Legal contextual factors that can influence the business) and the Market

Analysis. The PEST will also be a key piece of information that should be used when defining the Business Strategy; however, the Market Analysis is a key component that will be updated when defining the Business Strategy.

Then, the Business Plan will include an Internal Analysis, along with a SWOT Analysis (strengths, weaknesses, opportunities and threats for the company) and a PORTER Analysis of the competitive environment. Both exercises will be reused during the definition of the Business Strategy.

The following components of the Business Plan will also be taken into account for the Business Strategy. They are the Operations Plan (defining the Product and/or Service Lines, the Operational Model and the Organizational Model), the Marketing Plan, the Financial Plan and the Action Plan.

The last sections of the Business Plan will not be used to define the Strategy (the legal aspects and development team).

The following table summarizes the analyses to be performed. Read it in detail and ask any questions in the corresponding section:

Components of the Business Plan	Impact on the Business Strategy
Positioning	
Company's Mission	It is a relevant piece of information for the Business Strategy.
Company's Vision	It is a relevant piece of information for the Business Strategy.
Strategic Objectives	The Business Strategy must also be governed by these objectives. You will update these, if needed.
External Analysis	
PEST Factor Analysis	It is a relevant piece of information for the Business Strategy.
Market Analysis	Market Analysis is a key component that will be repeated/updated during the Business Strategy.
Internal Analysis	
SWOT Analysis	It is a relevant piece of information for the Business Strategy.
PORTER Analysis of the competitive environment	It is a relevant piece of information for the Business Strategy.
Operational Plan	
Product and/or service lines	The description of the product and/or service lines is relevant information for the Business Strategy. They will be updated in the Ansoff matrix.
Operating model	It is a relevant piece of information for the Business Strategy.
Organizational model	It is a relevant piece of information for the Business Strategy.
Marketing Plan	It is a relevant piece of information for the Business Strategy.
Action Plan	It is a relevant piece of information for the Business Strategy. It will be updated and new one will be created specifically for implementing the defined strategy.
Financial Plan	It is a relevant piece of information for the Business Strategy.
Legal Aspects	This is not used in the Business Strategy
Development Team	This is not used in the Business Strategy

As a result of these analyses, you can see that the Business Strategy is based on information from the Business Plan. However, these processes have only four axes of analysis in common: the Market Analysis, the description of the product/service lines, the Financial Plan, and the Action Plan.

This is why you should not confuse the Business Plan with the Business Strategy. From a practical point of view, they are two different strategic planning processes that pursue different objectives.

The method for developing the Business Strategy is described in detail below.

KEY BUSINESS OBJECTIVES

Let's start with the first activity of the Business Strategy—identifying the key objectives. The first thing we can ask ourselves is: Why should we start here? The answer is simply because the actions within the Business Strategy must be completely tailored toward reaching those objectives.

Imagine that a service company has decided to strengthen its outsourcing business at the expense of its consulting business. Normally, this decision is made in order to consolidate a company's long-term revenue. This is, therefore, one of its key strategic objectives. Can you think of an action that will achieve growth by strengthening the consulting business? Logically, no.

In the case of the Cyberlog study, aligning the defined strategy with the key business objectives was also clear. The Board's main objective was to renew growth, and a strategy was defined to do this, based mainly on the creation of a new business unit to sell a new cybersecurity product on SAP.

But how can you define key business objectives? Easy—in reality they are just a small number of medium-long-term goals pursued under the Business Strategy and fall under different perspectives:

—Finance: growth objectives (in the case of Cyberlog study, "to increase profitability up to an EBITDA of 16% over sales").

—Client: level of impact and relevance to our final customers (in the previous case of Cyberlog, "to increase market share from 2,460 to 3,500 customers").

—Internal: efficiency and effectiveness of internal operations (in the previous case of Cyberlog, the new CRM system).

—Talent: level of success in the managing people and work teams.

The fulfillment of these objectives should be measurable through different metrics, which must be simple, objective, and easy to understand. These are the so-called KPIs (which stands for *Key Performance Indicators*). When defining Business Strategies, the KPIs are metrics that will be used to measure the success of their implementation. In the case of Cyberlog, an example of KPI would be the EBITDA (it must be higher than 16% over sales after launching the strategy).

So, the first step of a Business Strategy is to define the key objectives and their KPIs. These objectives can be kept track of in the following table:

Perspective	Key Business Objectives	KPI	Threshold
Finance	.....	.....	
Client	.....	.....	
Internal	.....	.....	
Talent	...	.....	

The threshold is the target value that a KPI is expected to reach in a given period of time (the 16% from before). By comparing the expected results with actual results, it will be possible to conclude whether the Business Strategy is being successful or not. If not, corrective actions must be taken. Therefore, when implementing any Business Strategy, procedures should be created for reviewing compliance with key objectives. To do this, the value of the KPIs and their deviation from the established thresholds will be measured.

Let's take a look at a new example. Imagine a healthcare startup located in the UK that develops mobile health applications. Let's suppose that this startup is called HealthApp. Below are examples of what the key objectives of their business strategy might be and potential KPIs:

Perspective	Key Business Objectives	KPI	Threshold
Finance	Double-digit growth in the next three years	Sales/Revenue	15% annual growth
Client	Expand the customer base in hospitals	Number of hospitals using mobile applications	>=50
Internal	Reduce software test costs	Software testing costs	<20% of the final product
Talent	Increase programmers' satisfaction	Level of programmer satisfaction	>=95%

As you can see, objectives must be identified for all the business perspectives. Read the details of the example closely because HealthApp will be a case study that we will work with throughout the book.

Below are examples of typical key objectives for you to use when developing your own business strategy:

Perspective	Key Business Objectives	KPI	Threshold
Finance	Double the size of the business in the next five years	Sales and revenue	$40 million (double the current)
	Increase profitability in three basic areas in the next five years.	EBITDA	20% over sales
Client	Acquire new clients	Number of new clients	10 new clients each year
	Increase the level of customer satisfaction	Average customer satisfaction level	>=9.0
	Improve market positioning in the next three years.	% Market share	>=40%
Internal	Reduce procurement costs in the next two years	Purchase costs	2.5% reduction per year
	Greater efficiency of new product development	Time to market	<1 Year
Talent	Improve the level of employee satisfaction	Employee satisfaction level	>=9.5
	Improve employee skills	Training hours per employee	+170 hours

Makes a lot more sense now, right? However, before moving on to the next reading I want to propose an exercise. Can you define the key business objectives of a listed NASDAQ company? You don't need to write a 200-page document, I would be more than satisfied if you can identify 3 key objectives and their perspectives.

MARKET DATA ANALYSIS

Once we have defined the key business objectives, we must address the next BSB activity: the Market Analysis. To define a business strategy, it is necessary to first evaluate the context and the potential of the target market. In short, this means answering the question, "How is the market structured and what is our positioning?" by analyzing 10 key points:

1. What is the nature of the market we are operating in?
2. What are the main challenges for customers in this market?
3. Do these challenges open up new business opportunities?
4. What is the potential market size?
5. Is the market stable, growing, or shrinking?
6. What is our market share?
7. Who are our current customers and what do they buy?
8. Who are our "natural" customer segments?
9. What are our main products or services?
10. What is our position in relation to the competition?

Answering these questions is absolutely necessary for identifying the different Growth Drivers, the next step of the Business Strategy. Growth drivers must always respond to the customer's challenges identified during this analysis and should be aligned with the current positioning of the business.

To answer the questions posed above, we must carry out the following steps.

First, we will analyze primary sources of information; in other words, our own knowledge of the market, that of our company's experts, and that of our clients. For the latter, ask them what you want to find out from the Market

Analysis. For example, what is their agenda? What are their main challenges? What do they expect from your company? Focus on their challenges. You can collect this information using surveys, direct observation, or interviews. In general, it is best to use face-to-face interviews.

Once you have the client's point of view and your own, start checking other sources of information (called secondary sources). That is, databases, specialized publications, and market content. The Internet is a great source of secondary information. Learn everything you can about the evolution of the market in recent years. This information will allow you to predict the behavior of clients in the medium-long term. In some cases, it will also be necessary to buy market reports from research companies.

Let's continue with the HealthApp example, the Health startup located in the UK that develops mobile applications. Below is an example of what their Market Analysis might look like (the example shown is an executive summary from a Market Analysis that was really done).

First, let's talk about the nature of the market in which we operate. The Health market in the UK is managed by different actors: the public system (the leader in terms of revenue and is represented by the *National Health Service*) and the private one. In both sectors we have healthcare payers and healthcare providers.

Now let's turn to the main challenges facing clients that can be summarized as follows: managing chronic patients, low efficiency use of clinical resources, insufficient productivity of medical professionals, and the need to evolve towards proactive treatment where patients can make their own health decisions.

Do these challenges open up new business opportunities? The answer is yes. The potential contribution of mobile applications to solving these business challenges is evident. Examples of applications that can be sold are: mobile Electronic Health Record (EHR) solutions, mobile applications for chronic patient management, and mobile solutions for pharmaceutical companies.

In order to determine market size, we will use public reports from market researchers. All of them are saying that the global market for mobile applications in Healthcare has a potential of several billion dollars and is growing by double-digits each year (we should consider that our company has a market share of less than 1%).

In terms of customers, the NHS is the main one, representing 60% of our business. This organization mainly buys our solution to support clinical diagnoses.

In this sense, two applications currently account for 75% of our business: the application for managing chronic diabetes patients and the solution for patient diagnoses. Therefore, our client segment is naturally hospitals.

And, finally, we can say that our main competitors are consulting firms with healthcare verticals that offer their own developments to customers.

The following table summarizes the analysis performed:

1.	What is the nature of the market we are operating in?	Mostly public healthcare system (National Health Service, NHS)
2.	What are the main challenges for customers in this market?	Managing chronic patients, poor efficiency, insufficient productivity, and the need for moving towards proactive treatments.
3.	Do these challenges open up new business opportunities?	Yes. The potential contribution of mobile applications to solving the business challenges has grown substantially
4.	What is the potential market size?	Several Billions of dollars
5.	Is the market stable, growing, or shrinking?	Double digit growth
6.	What is our market share?	Less than 1%
7.	Who are our current customers and what do they buy?	The main client is the NHS (60% of our business) and mostly buys our solution for clinical diagnosis support.
8.	Who are our "natural" customer segments?	Our natural customer segment is hospitals.
9.	What are our main products or services?	Two applications currently account for 75% of our business: the application for managing chronic diabetes patients and the support solution for diagnosing patients.
10.	What is our position in relation to the competition?	Our main competitors are consulting firms with healthcare verticals.

As you can see, the Market Analysis allows us to figure out our starting point and helps to determine new products or services that we can sell as part of the Business Strategy.

Before moving on to the next reading, I want to propose an exercise. Create a Market Analysis for selling Artificial Intelligence solutions. As a secondary source of information, you can use public information from market researchers.

ORGANIC GROWTH DRIVERS

Once the key business objectives have been defined and the market context has been analyzed, we need to identify the strategies for achieving the defined growth objectives. These are the so-called growth drivers in the BSB.

There are two types of growth drivers: organic and inorganic. The organic, or internal, drivers are those that are based on current and/or future solutions from the company itself. The inorganic, or external, drivers rely on third parties through alliances, mergers, or acquisitions.

We will use the Ansoff matrix, also called the product-market matrix, to define the organic growth drivers. This matrix is one of the main business strategy and strategic marketing tools. It was created by strategist Igor Ansoff in 1957.

However, before explaining this matrix, I am going to talk about what a Market is. In practical terms, a market is a group of customers. For example, if we talk about entering a new insurance market, we are talking about either selling insurance directly or selling my product to insurance companies. If we talk about entering the Chinese market, we are talking about the set of potential customers in that country (whether they are companies and/or final consumers).

Well, now that we have clarified that, let's see how to develop the Ansoff matrix. This matrix is for relating products to markets, classifying the product-market binomial based on novelty or actuality. As a result, we get four quadrants with precise information on what is the best option to follow in order to achieve the greatest organic growth for the company.

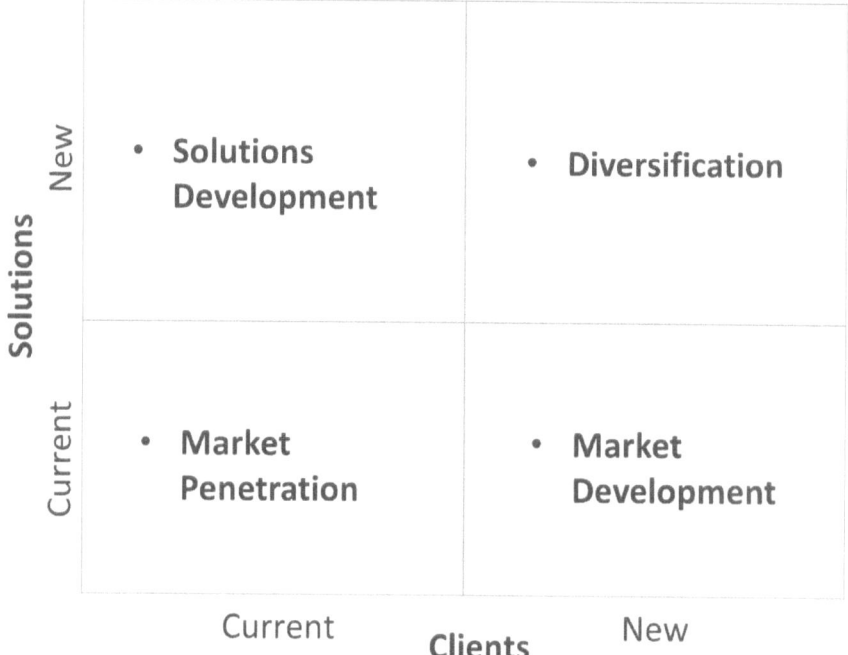

The first quadrant is for Existing Solutions with Existing Customers (also called Market Penetration). This means looking for growth through increasing sales of existing solutions with existing customers, through new sales techniques and/or more aggressive promotional and distribution tactics. This strategy, therefore, is to pursue increased share in existing markets by adapting existing solutions to respond to the challenges identified in the Market Analysis.

The second quadrant is for Existing Solutions with New Customers (also called Market Development). This means looking for growth by increasing sales of existing solutions with new customers. This strategy, therefore, entails expanding to new markets by adapting existing solutions to respond to the challenges the customers of those markets face.

The third quadrant is for New Solutions with Existing

Clients (also called Solution Development). This means looking for growth by the development of new solutions and selling them to existing customers.

The fourth and final quadrant is for New Solutions with New Customers (also called Diversification). This means growing by developing new solutions and selling them to new customers.

Next, I'll explain how to integrate these organic growth drivers into the Business Strategy.

MARKET PENETRATION

Let's start with the first quadrant: combining existing solutions and existing customers.

As part of the Business Strategy, the possibility of reaching the defined growth objectives must be analyzed in terms of increasing the existing solutions with the existing customers (increase in Market Penetration).

To do this, we must identify the existing solutions that can produce the greatest amount of growth in existing markets, analyzing them in two axes.

The first axis is market attractiveness. For this, we must assess the following variables for each growth driver:

—Estimated market size: has significant market potential.

—Operating margins: presents high margins.

—Level of competition: competition does not exist or can be easily beaten.

—Ability to differentiate: our value proposition is different from that of our competitors.

—Current and future positioning: we currently have decent positioning and can substantially improve in the future.

The second axis is the solution's feasibility and alignment with the business (Fit and Feasibility criteria).

For this, we must assess the following variables for each growth driver:

—Alignment with the company's current capabilities.

—Alignment with the key business objectives.

—Level of coverage for customers' challenges.

—Investment level required.

—Risk: the associated risks are minimal and/or manageable.

Think of HealthApp. Can we think about strengthening support for patient diagnoses using a mobile solution that currently exists? Definitely. This solution is aligned with the company's current capabilities and business objectives, which were the following:

Perspective	Key Business Objectives
Finance	Double-digit growth in the next three years
Client	Increase client base in hospitals
Internal	Reduce the costs of software testing
Talent	Increase programmer satisfaction

In particular, selling to new hospitals can allow us to expand our customer base. In addition, it offers a clear response to the challenges facing healthcare customers, especially in regard to increasing productivity and efficiency. Finally, there is a relevant market size (based on our findings in the Market Analysis, digital health has billions of dollars in potential). The same would apply to managing chronic diabetes patients.

Once we have determined that an existing solution-existing market combination can be a key task for the Business Strategy, we will classify it as:

—High potential: it is expected to support most of the growth in the coming years.

—Sustained growth: will have some impact on growth in the coming years.

—Flat growth: sales growth is not expected for the next few years.

—Not a priority: this solution-market combination will not be focused on (it could even be discontinued).

The following table summarizes this classification:

Classification	Market attractiveness	Fit and Feasibility with the Business
High potential	High	High
Sustained growth	Medium	High
Flat growth	Medium	Medium
Not a priority	Low	Low

Logically, the combinations characterized as "high potential" will be prioritized as part of the Business Strategy.

MARKET DEVELOPMENT

Let's now turn to the second quadrant: identifying areas for growth by combining existing solutions and new clients (Market Development).

More and more, businesses need to operate globally and internationally. On one hand, commercial barriers are being eliminated, which generates new business opportunities. On the other hand, new international competitors appear in local markets, which means that companies have to rethink their strategies. Additionally, in the face of possible global economic instability, becoming an international business has become a necessity for companies as an alternative to profitability, access to new clients, and growth.

With this in mind, the Business Strategy should analyze the possibility of reaching their growth metrics by expanding to new markets; in other words, selling existing solutions to new customers.

Therefore, once the key business objectives have been defined, the possibility of reaching the defined growth objectives must be analyzed in terms of increasing sales of the existing solutions with new customers.

In regard to geographic expansion, emerging markets currently offer the greatest possibilities for growth. In particular, these types of countries offer a very attractive potential given the high expected future growth (above 20%) and their desire to be at the same level of developed countries, fostering a favorable business climate.

China, with more than one billion consumers, is an excellent market to expand (remember the case of Apple).

South America has had substantial growth of its income per capita, allowing for the population to develop higher professional qualifications, as well as the establishment of new commercial frameworks at the institutional level, increasing business stability and decreasing risk.

Africa is an untapped market, with large needs for importing all kinds of goods and services for its full development. The European and American governments' growing interest is favors establishing multilateral agreements with countries of this continent, which gives security to trade agreements.

And, finally, there is India, where access to a large-volume potential market is of great interest.

To conclude and give you an idea of the importance of geographic expansion, I will tell you that the United States is the second largest economy in the world in terms of exports. According to the World Bank, its exports amounted to $1.45 trillion in 2016.

Therefore, we must value all these markets—and others—in order to identify the new customer bases where we can expand the business and we can classify the solution-market combination just as we did before (high potential, sustained growth, flat growth, not a priority).

Classification	Market attractiveness	Fit and Feasibility with the Business
High potential	High	High
Sustained growth	Medium	High
Flat growth	Medium	Medium
Not a priority	Low	Low

As an example, let's go back to our healthcare startup. Did you know that—according to data from Market Researchers—China, India, and Japan will lead the mobile applications market in healthcare for Pacific Asia? We could establish an agreement with a local partner to maximize the viability of the operation. Therefore, it does not seem a bad idea to expand into these markets.

Once again, the combinations characterized as "high potential" will be prioritized as part of the Business Strategy.

SOLUTION DEVELOPMENT

Now let's turn to the third quadrant: identifying areas of growth based on the combination of new solutions and existing customers (Solution Development).

Developing new solutions is a key element in defining the Business Strategy because innovation is one of the biggest influences on profitable growth. Therefore, we must now analyze the possibility of reaching the growth metrics defined in the Business Strategy by creating new solutions to sell to existing clients.

The business strategy team should design new, distinguishable solutions that are aligned with the criterion for market attractiveness and feasibility which I explained previously.

Once a new solution and its corresponding market has been identified, we will document it as part of the strategy.

First, there is your Value Proposition—in other words, what you will offer as part of the solution and what makes you different from the competition. However, this definition is very nuanced. It is actually better to say that the Value Proposition is what makes you different and what your client is willing to pay for. This is a key point for defining any new solution. Many people believe that they have the idea of the century, but they realize too late that no client is willing to pay for it.

And, finally, you have the alignment of the new solution with the identified business challenges.

Once the solution-market combinations have been defined and documented, they should be prioritized according to the criteria we went over previously:

Classification	Market attractiveness	Fit and Feasibility
High potential	High	High
Sustained growth	Medium	High
Flat growth	Medium	Medium
Not a priority	Low	Low

Logically, the combinations characterized as "high potential" will be prioritized as part of the Business Strategy.

Think about HealthApp. Can you think of new solutions to sell to current UK customers? In the Market Analysis we have already seen an example: Electronic Health Record mobile solutions.

DIVERSIFICATION

Let's finish with the fourth quadrant: combining new solutions with new customers.

As part of the Business Strategy, the possibility of reaching the defined growth objectives must be analyzed in terms of creating new solutions to sell to new clients (Diversification).

To do this, you will repeat the process we went over in the previous reading, but this time thinking about new potential customers we can expand to.

As a result of this analysis, the new solutions/new clients will prioritized according to the following criteria:

Classification	Market attractiveness	Fit and Feasibility
High potential	High	High
Sustained growth	Medium	High
Flat growth	Medium	Medium
Not a priority	Low	Low

Logically, the combinations characterized as "high potential" will be prioritized as part of the Business Strategy.

Let's think about HealthApp again. Can you think of new solutions to sell to new clients? We identified one earlier: mobile solutions for pharmaceutical companies (new customers).

HOW TO DOCUMENT ORGANIC GROWTH DRIVERS

In this section, we will see how the drivers of organic growth that have been identified as part of the Business Strategy should be documented.

First, you will include a table with the detailed list of possible drivers of organic growth that you have identified. For this, the following template will be used:

Organic Growth Driver	New Clients	Value Proposition	Alignment with the client's business challenges	Type of Driver
Existing Solutions/Existing Clients				
Name	N/A	...	...	...
Existing Solutions/New Clients				
Name	...	...	...	...
New Solutions/Existing Clients				
Name	N/A	...	...	...
New Solutions/New Clients				
Name	...	...	...	...

In other words, you will detail how each growth driver will affect new customers/markets (for those based on existing customers, this will be "not applicable"), the value proposition, the level of alignment with customer challenges that you have identified, and which category it falls under (High potential, Sustained growth, Flat growth, or Not a priority).

After that, you will include a graph of all the organic growth drivers according to the Ansoff matrix.

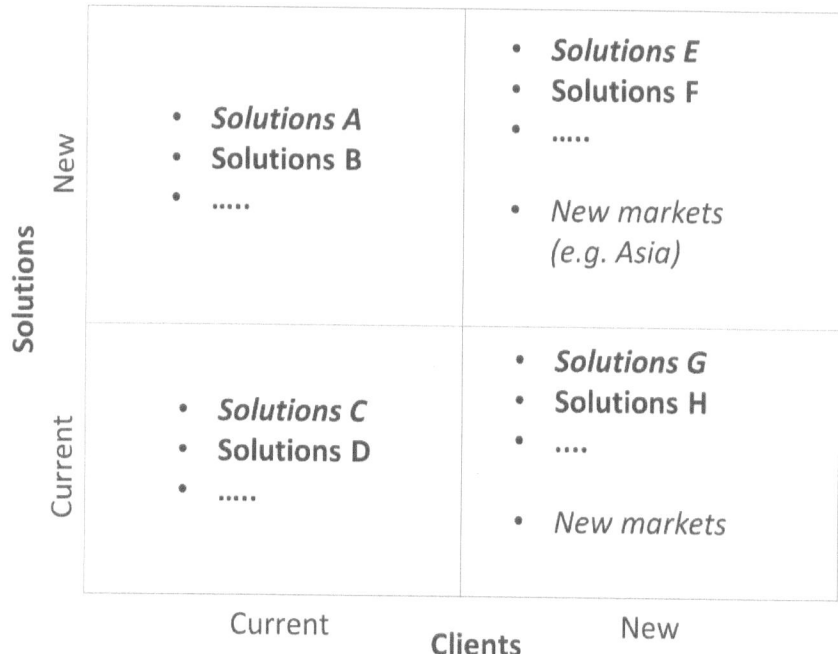

- **High potential**: it is expected to support most of the growth in the coming years.
- **Sustained growth**: will have some impact on growth in the coming years.

Then, you will include a summary of how the organic growth drivers align with the identified challenges (so that you can be sure that all of the client's challenges are covered, or so you can identify other possible opportunities).

Once the organic growth drivers have been documented, you will make a detailed definition for those that have been categorized as "High potential" or "Sustained growth." The objective of this exercise is to make it easier to understand the key growth strategies that have been selected.

To do this, you will first show the name and description of the driver next to the financial forecasts that justify its categorization. This will detail the expected sales, revenue, and margins in the coming years:

x $1000	Year 1	Year 2	Year 3	Year 4	Year 5
Sales & Revenue Total	0,000	0,000	0,000	0,000	0,000
Margin %	0%	0%	0%	0%	0%

Next, you will present the list of KPIs that were defined for the Key Business Objectives that will be impacted by this driver (and we will use this to measure the success of the Business Strategy).

Then, you will provide information about the customers.

—Target Customers

—Opportunities in Progress

—Level of competition: a general reflection on our competitors—"What will they do to beat us?" and "What will we do to beat them?"

Finally, you will develop the Action Plan needed in order to implement the high priority drivers of organic growth. This plan will be part of the Business Strategy's overall implementation plan, which I will explain later.

ORGANIC GROWTH DRIVERS: HEALTHAPP EXAMPLE

Let's develop and document the organic growth drivers for HealthApp as an example. Remember that the company operates in the UK and two applications account for 75% of its current business: an application for managing chronic diabetes patients and a support solution for diagnosing patients.

As a result of the Market Analysis, we also discovered that the client's main challenges were the managing chronic patients, the low efficiency use of clinical resources, the insufficient productivity levels of medical professionals, and the need to evolve towards proactive treatments where patients can make their own healthcare decisions.

Let's start with a table summarizing the drivers of organic growth. After completing the analysis, we are left with the following conclusions:

Organic Growth Driver	New Clients	Value Proposition	Alignment with the client's business challenges	Type of Driver
Existing Solutions/Existing Clients				
Application for managing chronic diabetes patients	N/A	Improving the quality of life and efficiency of diagnosing patients with diabetes	It covers all identified challenges, especially chronicity	Sustained growth
Support solution for patient diagnosis.	N/A	Optimizing the costs of making diagnoses through the use of Artificial Intelligence	Improving the efficiency of resource utilization and the productivity of medical professionals	Sustained growth
Existing Solutions/New Clients				
Geographic expansion of existing solutions	Expanding to China and the U.S.	See above	See above	High potential

Organic Growth Driver	New Clients	Value Proposition	Alignment with the client's business challenges	Type of Driver
New Solutions/Existing Clients				
EHR Mobile Solutions	N/A	The new EHR mobile solution will reduce the saturation of the healthcare system	It covers all identified challenges, especially those regarding efficiency	High potential
New Solutions/New Clients				
EHR Mobile Solutions	China and USA	Optimizing healthcare costs and process improvement	It covers all identified challenges, especially those regarding efficiency	High potential
Mobile solution for pharmaceutical companies	Pharmaceutical companies	Improve the efficiency of diagnosis	Proactive medicine	Not a priority

As the table shows, the analysis has determined the organic growth drivers, which are represented below in the corresponding Ansoff matrix:

- *High Potential*
- *Sustained growth*
- Flat growth
- <u>Not a priority</u>

In other words, we have four drivers with high potential for organic growth: expanding current solutions to China/USA (2) and creating a new EHR solution for current and new markets (2).

We also have drivers that fall under sustained growth (the support solution for diagnosing patients for existing clients), flat growth (the application for managing chronic diabetes patients for existing clients), and a new solution that has been determined as non-priority (the mobile solution for the pharmaceutical industry).

As you can see, it is not as difficult as it seems. If you were the CEO of this company and you had to communicate your strategy to investors, you could say the following: *"We expect sustained growth for our solutions in today's markets. However, we believe that we can double our business over the next five years by selling our existing solutions in China and the USA, as well as creating a mobile solution for electronic health records (EHR). These solutions respond to the current challenges facing the healthcare system in terms of efficiency, effectiveness, and quality."*

Next, we will make a summary of how the solutions align with the challenges facing the client that we have identified (so that we can verify that our solution portfolio offers answers to all the client's challenges).

	Application for managing chronic diabetes patients	Support solution for patient diagnosis	EHR Solution	Mobile solution for data analysis
Managing chronic patients	X		X	
Efficient use of clinical resources	X	X	X	
Productivity of medical professionals	X	X	X	
Proactive medicine	X		X	X

From this table, we can conclude that we correctly identified all of the organic growth drivers given that, from a global perspective, they are aligned with all the customer challenges we identified (i.e. HealthApp is able to offer solutions to customers in order to manage all of the identified challenges).

Finally, you'll make a detailed definition of the organic

growth drivers that have been classified as "High Potential" or "Sustained Growth."

Let's look at an example of one of them: selling an Electronic Health Record (EHR) solution in China and the U.S. (new solution with new customers).

First, here's the description of the solution: "mobile access to Hospital Information Systems by healthcare professionals, patients, and clients/citizens."

Subsequently, here is the sales, revenue, and profitability estimate for the coming years:

x $1000	Year 1	Year 2	Year 3	Year 4	Year 5
Revenue	1,000	3,000	5,000	6,000	12,000
Margin %	28%	36%	42%	43%	45%

As we can see, this driver has a high potential for growth, which justifies its categorization.

Next, we will include a description of the KPIs defined for the Key Business Objectives that will be impacted by this solution (which we will use to measure the success of the Business Strategy). Remember that they were as follows:

Perspective	Key Business Objectives	KPI	Threshold	Example of impact
Finance	Double-digit growth over the next three years	Revenue	15% annual growth	7% will come from the new solution
Client	Expand the customer base in hospitals	Number of hospitals using mobile applications	>=50	10 new customers in current markets, 3 in China, and 5 in the U.S.

As we can see in the table, this organic growth driver will allow for 7% growth (financial KPI) and will bring in 8 new clients in the U.S. and China combined.

Next, we will provide information about the customers.

Element	Content
Target Customers	Private hospitals in China and the U.S.
Opportunities in Progress	Those identified by the local team.
Level of Competition	Other local digital healthcare solution providers with more licensing in the country and/or that are cheaper than ours.

Finally, we will include the action plan needed for implementing this organic growth driver. Remember that this plan will be part of the Business Strategy's global implementation plan, which I will explain later.

As you may have seen in this exercise, the process of reflecting on and documenting the organic growth drivers for the Business Strategy allows us to determine the paths of growth based on the sale of our portfolio of products and services (existing and new) to our customers (existing and new).

Next, we will discuss the following step of the BSB method: identifying inorganic growth drivers. However, before we do this, I want to pose a challenge for you: would you be able to prepare a presentation for investors on the new EHR solution, including the qualitative and quantitative aspects of it?

INORGANIC GROWTH DRIVERS

Let's now go to the next step of the process: identifying the inorganic growth drivers.

This so-called inorganic (or external) growth comes from the participation, merger, or acquisition of third-party companies, as opposed to using the company's own solutions.

This type of growth helps companies to:

—Enter into new markets (for example, it is easier to expand to China by establishing an alliance or buying a company from that country).

—Expand the current client base (for example, capturing the clients of the company with which we have merged).

—Reduce competition (for example, if we acquire a stake in or merge with a competitor). Later we will see an example of this.

—Grow quickly (when "acquiring" the revenue of the other company).

—Use new technology (what big technology companies usually do when they buy high-tech startups).

The following are the types of inorganic growth that you can use as part of your Business Strategy:

—Acquisition: one company buys another without forming a new one.

—Fusion: two companies combine to form a new one.

—"Joint Venture": business relationship in which the partners create a new business and share the risks and benefits according to agreed upon terms and conditions.

—Strategic partnership: partnership with a company to jointly develop a part of the Business Strategy.

As you can imagine, the implementing inorganic growth drivers is a complex process with limited success rates. A clear example of its complexity was HP's purchase of Compaq. In 2001, HP bought Compaq for $33 billion, becoming the world's largest manufacturer of home computers. The objective was to reduce competition by eliminating a major competitor. However, HP's stock market value fell by half after the acquisition and, years later, Walter Hewlett deemed the inorganic growth strategy to be "an error."

In any case, as part of your Business Strategy, you should contemplate potential drivers of inorganic growth. As with organic growth, you must identify the following key pieces of information for each of them:

—Name of the inorganic growth driver.
—Description of the inorganic growth driver.
—Identify the key business objectives/KPIs that will be impacted by said inorganic growth driver.
—Business case, including the operation costs and the expected qualitative/quantitative benefits.
—Action plan for implementation. This action plan must be high level and include the steps needed for putting the inorganic growth driver in place (and will be part of the Global Action Plan, which will described in later sections).

For example, the high-level action plan for HealthApp to successfully develop an inorganic growth process in China would be:

—Define the acquisition strategy: for example, we need to buy a mobile health solutions company in China, valued at less than $10 million.
—Identify candidates and prioritize: look for high-potential health technology startups and select the best ones.
—Develop qualitative assessments on target candidates: ease of integration, alignment between companies, etc.
—Develop preliminary financial valuations on target

candidates: quantify preliminary costs and revenues of the operation. Use standard business valuation methods to financially value the selected startups.

—Select the final candidate and develop due diligence: select the best startup and analyze it based on the different axes (financial, legal, labor, and fiscal, among others).

—Conduct due diligence: verify the value of the acquisition and review the strategy.

—Negotiate agreements and execute the acquisition.

As you can see, implementing an inorganic growth strategy is not an easy task. Not all companies are prepared for it. However, it is something that is done on a regular basis. To give you an idea, according to Thomson Reuters data, the volume of M&A operations in the U.S. from 2016 to 2018 has reached $1.2 trillion, and approximately 12,700 transactions have been carried out.

Finally, before moving on to the next section, I will leave you the below template, which you should use to document the drivers of inorganic growth:

Component	Description
Name	Name of the inorganic growth driver
Description	Description of the inorganic growth driver
Business Case	Summary of the case, including the costs of the operation and the expected qualitative/quantitative benefits
Alignment with the Key Business Objectives	What Key Business Objectives/KPIs will be affected by this organic growth driver?
Action Plan	Actions needed to implement the driver

ENABLERS

Now let's look at the next step of the BSB process: identifying the Enablers.

Enablers are actions that affect the entire company and create the capabilities needed to achieve the non-financial business objectives. They are called Enablers because, together with the Growth Drivers, they make the Business Strategy a reality.

Below, you can see examples of Enablers (in later sections, you will see many real examples of Enablers as part of the case studies):

—Have an IT platform that supports the new international expansion processes.

—Create a department responsible for the Digital Transformation of the Company (something that Nike did in 2010).

—Develop a talent management project to maximize team motivation.

—Install a culture of Performance Management, etc.

For the Business Strategy, the key characteristics for each Enabler will be defined:

Component	Description
Description	Description of the Enabler
Alignment with the Key Business Objectives	What Key Business Objectives/KPIs will be affected by this Enabler?
Alignment with the Growth Drivers	What Growth Drivers will be impacted by this Enabler?
Action Plan	The action plan must be high-quality and include the steps necessary for implementing the Enabler (and will be part of the Global Action Plan, which will be described in later sections).

In the next section, we will see how to come up with a one-page Business Strategy that is easy to understand and clearly communicates what it is intended to.

THE ONE PAGE BUSINESS STRATEGY

So far, we have seen how to identify the Key Business Objectives, perform a Market Analysis in order to find the challenges our customers face, and define the organic and inorganic growth drivers as well as the Enablers needed to achieve the desired objectives.

Once all this information has been obtained, it is advisable to represent it graphically in a way that allows us to understand it better, communicate it internally, and develop a detailed Financial Model and Global Action Plan.

To do this, you will use the following one-page Business Strategy template:

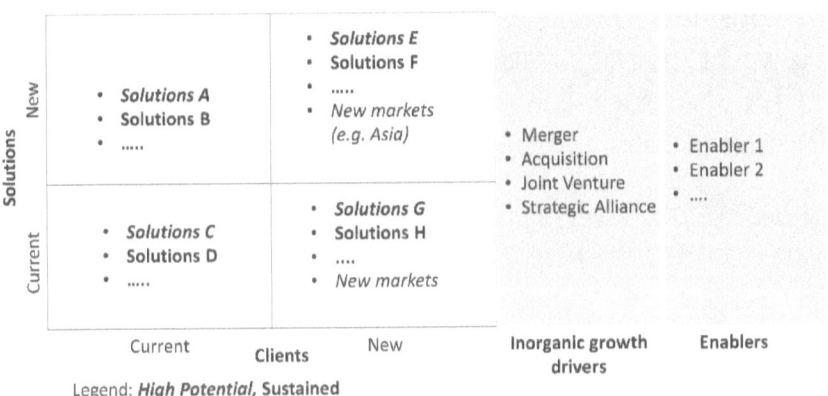

As you can see, the graph includes the following information:

—Organic Growth Drivers (according to the guidelines we have previously explained). Only those that are categorized as High potential or Sustained Growth (i.e. those that can offer the highest growth rates and, therefore, require potential investments) are included.

—Inorganic Growth Drivers

—Enablers

In the coming sections, we will show you real examples

of Business Strategies for different listed companies. However, before proceeding to these readings, I would like to propose a challenge. Do you want to try to draft the Business Strategy for HealthApp, our case study?

BUSINESS STRATEGY IN THE REAL WORLD

In this section, we will analyze real examples of Business Strategies together. To do this, we will work with different companies and analyze their activity and the key pieces of information from their Business Strategy. We will rely on data from the company's corporate website and public documents showing the company's somewhat recent financial reports.

Once all the information has been analyzed, we will move on to interpreting it; that is, we will reconstruct the actual business strategy of the company we are studying. Although, we will usually not be able to identify the company's entire business strategy, the analysis will sufficiently bring all the concepts together.

Finally, we will make a one-page graphic representation of the Business Strategy according to the template provided earlier.

Let's start with Stratasys. According to its website, this company "is a world leader in 3D printing — and its biggest fan. We are passionate believers in the value and power of 3D printing, and in the change it can bring to the world. We create the systems, materials and communities that make 3D printing essential for manufacturers, empowering for designers and educators, and inspiring for makers".

According to available information, to reach the Key Business Objectives in financial terms, the Company has proposed an organic growth strategy based on the development of new solutions for existing and new customers. An example would be selling MakerBot (a 3D printer for home use that was purchased by Stratasys) to final consumers (something that is not easy for manufacturers of 3D printers). Another example would be verticalization, like the creation of specific solutions for the health sector.

When it comes to inorganic growth drivers, both Stratasys and its main competitor, 3D Systems, have always been very active in this area. In other words, the company's strategy includes the development of strategic alliances with industry leaders and with customers.

Once we have identified the drivers of organic and inorganic growth, we can take look at the Enablers.

There are different types, although most of them refer to the need to align resources with market conditions and/or executing plans in order to significantly improve operations. In 2015, the Company began to struggle because its growth rates did not meet the expectations of investors (which also led to a sharp drop in their shares). Therefore, they switched to a strategy focused on improving profitability until market conditions changed, which ultimately meant costs optimization.

The one-page graphic representation of the Business Strategy would be as follows:

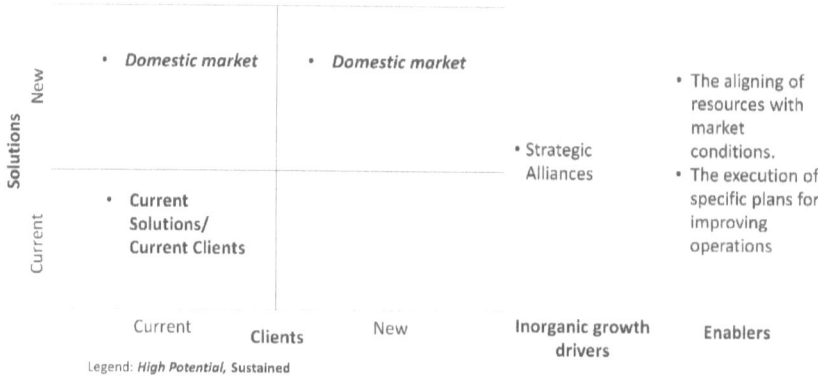

As you can see in the graph, the Company wants to obtain a significant part of its growth by protecting and expanding the current business through organic growth strategies based on selling the new printing solution in the domestic market.

Additionally, it is considering inorganic growth strategies based on alliances with third parties, especially with aerospace customers.

Finally, the Enablers that will also support the Key Business Objectives are the aligning of resources with market conditions and the execution of specific plans for improving operations.

It must be said that, to date, the Company focuses a large part of its current business strategy on verticalization, strengthening the domestic market (where the real hypergrowth may be possible), inorganic growth, and streamlining its operating costs. ☐

Let's move to Coca Cola. According to experts, 94% of the planet recognizes Coca Cola, so I don't think it's necessary to go over what the company does...

According to available information, to reach the Key Business Objectives in financial terms, the Company has two main drivers of growth. First, there is the development of new products for current customers that include more "Sugar-Free" options and smaller packaging. Second, there is the improvement of current products for new and existing customers.

In terms of inorganic growth, The Company plans to encourage mergers and acquisitions.

Once we have identified the drivers of organic and inorganic growth, we can look at the Enablers. The Company is very explicit about its strategy in relation to this point. In particular, they make reference to develop marketing campaigns to reposition the brand.

The one-page graphic representation of the Business Strategy would be as follows:

Let's continue with Netflix. According to its website, the Company "is the world's leading Internet television network with over 86 million members in over 190 countries enjoying more than 125 million hours of TV shows and movies per day, including original series, documentaries and feature films".

Being a company with a subscription business model, its main objective is to grow the number of users worldwide. In order to meet these objectives, the Company has developed organic growth drivers as a fundamental part of their business. Specifically, new products (original content and adding new languages such as Korean or Chinese) and expansion into new markets (China, for example).

Now that we have identified the drivers of growth, let's look at the Enablers.

There are many different types, although most of them focus on helping grow their number of subscriptions. For example, giving customers the ability to use international credit cards, to subscribe directly using a mobile phone, etc.

As such, the one-page graphic representation of the

Business Strategy would be as follows:

I hope you liked the case studies. In any case, remember that the goal is to sum up everything you have learned so far.

Now we are going to continue with the last steps for formulating the Business Strategy: defining the Financial Model and the Global Action Plan.

However, before we move on, I want to present a new challenge, and it's about Lego. In 2000, this company was in a major crisis. However, a few years later it had managed to overcome this situation and return to being a successful company (it currently brings in more than $5 billion a year). Can you come up with the Business Strategy they used to do this? It is not very hard, and it is also widely available on the Internet.

FINANCIAL MODEL

In this section, we are going to study a key step in the BSB process: defining the financial model, or the set of investments needed to implement the Business Strategy and the expected return.

Although the Financial Model of the Business Strategy is considerably simpler than the one developed in the Business Plan (as I have explained in previous sections), it is a crucial step for correctly executing the defined strategy.

In this sense, the Financial Model must determine the investments needed in order to develop the Business Strategy, the expected financial benefits (which must be aligned with those established in the KPIs), and the associated risks.

To develop the Financial Model, you will complete the following activities.

First, you must determine the focus of the analysis, which should be approved by the Business Strategy team and the company's key decision makers.

Next, you will develop a working hypothesis that will guide the entire analysis.

Then, based on this hypothesis, you will determine what investments needed to implement the Strategy. These investments must sufficiently cover the financial requirements of human resources, marketing and operations, among others.

You will also calculate the growth that is expected as a result of implementing the Business Strategy in terms of sales, revenue, and profitability.

Once the investments and returns have been determined, you will complete a sensitivity analysis; in other words, you will determine the risk of not reaching the targets if there are changes made to the hypothesis.

Finally, you will document the conclusions and recommendations from the Financial Model so that they can be reviewed by the Board of Directors.

Let's look at an example of a Financial Model using our startup, HealthApp. We'll consider the opportunity for organic growth based on "creating a new mobile EHR solution."

Let's start with the working hypothesis. We are going to assume that this solution will only be sold in the UK (we do not know enough the legislation of the health market in the U.S. and we prefer to postpone selling it in this market). As you will see below, this hypothesis will have an impact on the expected benefits calculation.

Next, we must determine the investments we will need to implement this Growth Driver. Logically, in order to create the new app, we must invest in talent, software, hardware, etc. This investment should be included in the Financial Model, as shown in the following table:

x $1000	Year 1	Year 2	Year 3	Year 4	Year 5
UK Revenue					
Investments	1,000	1,560			
Other costs	250	400	700	750	800
Margin %					
U.S. Revenue	0	0	0	0	0
Margin %	0%	0%	0%	0%	0%

Let's now calculate the expected growth from implementing this organic growth driver in terms of revenue and profitability. It might look something like the following:

x $1000	Year 1	Year 2	Year 3	Year 4	Year 5
UK Revenue	1,000	2,000	3,000	4,000	4,500
Investments	1,000	1,560			
Other costs	250	400	700	750	800
Margin %	-25%	2%	77%	81%	82%
U.S. Revenue	0	0	0	0	0
Margin %	0%	0%	0%	0%	0%

As you can see, in the Financial Model, we estimated that sales in the U.S. will be zero in the next few years (this was our main hypothesis).

What would be the sensitivity analysis in this Financial Model? We could play around with a few different variables. For example, if we expand to the U.S., revenue will change substantially (although we will take on legal risks). We can also analyze the amount of sensitivity to the cost of developing the solution (logically, higher costs means lower margins).

Next, we will see the last step of the process: developing the Global Action Plan that will guide the Business Strategy implementation.

GLOBAL ACTION PLAN

The time has come to develop the Action Plan for implementing the strategy and achieving the key business objectives. As I explained before, this plan should include the tasks identified throughout the strategic planning process; that is, actions associated with the drivers of organic and inorganic growth and the Enablers.

The different components of the plan will be classified according to their nature into:

—Actions related to Leadership.
—Actions related to the Business.
—Actions related to People.
—Actions related to Marketing & Media.

Continuing with the HealthApp example, the following could possibly be the Action Plan for their Business Strategy.

First, there are the actions related to the Leadership:

—Define the department and the team responsible for leading the Business Strategy implementation.
—Choose the business leaders for the new countries (USA and China) and for the new solutions.

Then, there are the actions related to the Business:

—Build the new EHR solution.
—Develop a detailed plan for expanding to China and the U.S.
—Identify possible local allies in both countries.
—Identify and execute possible acquisitions of companies in both countries.

Next, there are the actions related to People:

—Plan and execute a meeting to communicate the new Business Strategy to the employees.
—Contract programmers that specialize in EHR mobile

solutions.

And, finally, there are the Marketing & Media actions:

—Marketing campaign for the new EHR solution.

—Marketing Campaign in Digital Healthcare for U.S. and China.

—Participate in key healthcare events in both countries.

The following template can be used to document the Global Action Plan:

Action	Type	Responsible	Due Date
Define the department and the team responsible for leading the Business Strategy implementation.	Leadership	…..	…..
Develop a detailed plan for expanding to China and the U.S.	Business	…..	….
Plan and execute a meeting to communicate the new Business Strategy to the employees.	People	….	….
Marketing campaign for the new EHR solution.	Marketing	….	….
…..	….	…	….

In the event that you work for a corporation, you will most likely submit the Action Plan to the Board so that, once approved, a team will be created that will then be responsible for implementing it, which you will surely be part of (and possibly even lead it).

If you work for a startup, what you would do is discuss it with the owners so that, once approved, you will lead the implementation with a slightly smaller team (or even on your own).

The way you execute the Action Plan can be more or less complicated depending on its complexity. Actually, putting the Business Strategy in place is like starting a project. Therefore, most of the time, you must apply Project Management techniques to ensure its success.

Normally, companies have their own Project Management processes that you can follow to implement the Global Action Plan. Startups will likely use an "Agile" approach and corporations a "Predictive" approach; in any case, use the following recommendations to help you successfully implement the Business Strategy:

—Assign a leader to be accountable for the plan's execution.

—Anticipate how the new strategy will affect the company's employees, processes, and culture.

—Regularly communicate the status and results of the strategy implementation.

— Review the progress of the plan on a quarterly basis (at a minimum). Focus on the level of compliance with the key business objectives identified when the strategy was defined.

—Adapt the plan in case of non-compliance with objectives.

—Update the plan and live it!

In the next section, we will solve the Kodak puzzle that I presented at the beginning. Are you ready?

THE ANSWER TO THE KODAK PROBLEM

In the first reading, I posed a challenge. Do you remember what it was? It was as follows: In 2001, 3.12 billion rolls of photo film were sold worldwide. At that time, Kodak had a 40% market share, Fuji had 26% and Agfa had 13%; however, in 2012, only 11 years later, Kodak filed for bankruptcy. Can you tell me why?

As we saw in the sections that followed, one of the main steps in creating the Business Strategy is to understand our clients and their challenges. In the case of Kodak, their customers no longer just wanted a family photo album on the living room table, but the ability to take thousands of photos, delete a portion, and share the rest on the Internet.

Even though Kodak invented the first digital camera (it was created by one of its engineers, Steven Sasson), instead of offering it to their customers, they decided to protect it with a patent to prevent the invention from impacting their analog business. In other words, they went against their customers' wishes and that was the beginning of its decline.

On the other hand, another step in creating the Business Strategy is to analyze the competition. Being a leader in the photography industry for decades with more than 80% penetration in the United States, a market with a rate of return greater than 70%, Kodak did not want to accept that digital photography had brought new competitors that were going to reduce their market share. But, of course, they did appear and they did surpass them.

Finally, Kodak resisted changing his business model. This model was inspired by the so-called "Gillette model," in which a company sells the initial product (the camera) at a cheap price and the spare parts (photo rolls) that have a higher profit margin at a more expensive one. Throughout its existence, Kodak had virtually given away the cameras and charged a very high price for the chemicals needed for the development process. With the popularization of digital photography, that business model was out and Kodak did not realize it.

By the time the company decided to change its business strategy and join the world of digital photography, mobile phones with cameras had appeared—in other words, Kodak changed its organic growth strategy too late.

Something similar happened with emerging markets (new customers that follow organic growth). While companies from other industries managed to grow in countries such as China, Brazil and India, Kodak found that this was not possible (the emerging countries had jumped straight to using digital cameras, without ever using rolls of film).

As a result, the once ground-breaking photography company that was founded by George Eastman in the late nineteenth century declared bankruptcy in 2012 with billions of dollars in debt. Although the firm had tried to restructure, it had not been able to do so. In the third quarter of 2011 (the last period in which information was made available before the bankruptcy), Kodak lost more than $200 million. Its annual revenue came in around $6 billion, which just a little more than a third of what it made at its peak.

CONCLUSION

We have reached the end of the book. I hope you have enjoyed it.

If this book has been useful to you, I would sincerely appreciate it if you would leave a positive review online. This will allow other readers to be able to find it, since Google and Amazon sort authors based on the ratings they receive.

ABOUT THE AUTHOR

Bert is a private investor with experience in creating disruptive business models based on new technology trends. Throughout the last 15 years, he has dedicated himself mainly to coming up with business models for listed companies and helping tech startups move from the initial investment stage to the growth stage.

Get some of Bert's Popular Highly Recommended Books:

—*Blockchain for Business: A Hands-on approach:* Understand the Technical Principles of Blockchain, and learn how to build Successful Business Models based on this technology

—*Building Successful Business Models based on Artificial Intelligence:* Growing your Business Quickly using Machine Learning and Deep Learning

—*Create a Winning Digital Strategy:* Learn to create Successful Digital Strategies to boost Growth

—*Create a Winning Business Strategy:* Learn to create Successful Business Strategies to boost Growth